AN
ANGEL
THAT FELL, THAT SAVED A
BOY
FROM HELL

'Unveiling The Wings of Redemption: A Fallen Angel's
Salvation of a Boy's Transcendence From Hell'

JONATHAN SHAW

Gotham Books

30 N Gould St.
Ste. 20820, Sheridan, WY 82801
https://gothambooksinc.com/

Phone: 1 (307) 464-7800

© 2024 *Jonathan Shaw*. All rights reserved.

No part of this book may be reproduced, stored in a retrieval system, or transmitted by any means without the written permission of the author.

Published by Gotham Books (January 12, 2024)

ISBN: 979-8-88775-666-0 (H)
ISBN: 979-8-88775-664-6 (P)
ISBN: 979-8-88775-665-3 (E)

Because of the dynamic nature of the Internet, any web addresses or links contained in this book may have changed since publication and may no longer be valid.

The views expressed in this work are solely those of the author and do not necessarily reflect the views of the publisher, and the publisher hereby disclaims any responsibility for them.

TABLE OF CONTENTS

Interception from man's deception 1

I was one of thee, creation of the three 3

They call it a Start with half a heart 5

Awaiting Freedoms answers imprisoned in the mind 8

High Hopes for A Boys dream While being confined Down in Hells gleam 10

The Foul Grimy Room 13

Venom In the Vein 15

Mending the mental bridge 18

Be all ears hearkened to feelings some fear 20

When the subconscious mind awakens 23

Where the hearts at 26

Forever A wanderer accompanied by strangers 28

Scrolls to My Dear Angel 30

Enslavement In a lover's consciousness 32

Wounded 35

Learning to let go and be free like a child's glow 38

Turning Of the Tide Wrong To Right " 41

Connections from afar that transform through a metamorphosis Jar 45

My #sunshine 47

MY NAME IS SHAME 48

Intertwined by the vineyards vine 49

Epilogue 50

PREFACE

Most of these poems are based on actual experiences I've encountered, not only with love and redemption, but also with addictions, pain, and chaos. I use a lot of metaphoric speech and philosophy in my style of poetry to express my thoughts, emotions, and the actual experiences I've encountered in this life. The first two poems were found in my dreams, while the rest are events that occurred on my road to redemption, from meeting my blue-eyed angel to encountering my creator, to whom I dedicate this poetry book.

For the readers about to embark on reading this book, remember one famous poetry quote from Edgar Allan Poe, from whom I draw most of my inspiration: "Deep into that darkness peering, long I stood there, wondering, fearing, doubting, dreaming dreams no mortal ever dared to dream before."

INTERCEPTION FROM MAN'S DECEPTION

{Written by Jonathan Shaw}

Intercepting transmissions, I receive and send,
To achieve my purpose, I need more time to extend,
Connected with the seven stars inside of me,
Aligned from root to crown, a divine decree.

Discipline is the key to attain this holy seed,
Resisting temptation means shedding greed,
The Sandman knows my wisdom and insight,
Our first encounter in a parallel light.

Dimensions entwined, tying Earth's fabric,
Some mysteries best left to the minds with tactic,
slowly dripping away like a faucet's drip,
Speed of light, in constant cosmic slip.

The galaxies acknowledge Sandman's control,
Over the flow of secrets that speak to the soul,
our second encounter lit up the entity sphere,
A magnificent space firework, crystal clear.

Now I surrender to the need for more time,
Where mortals transform, immortals divine,
A curse disguised as a gift, wrapped in a bow,
For knowledge means truth, did you not know?

The Sandman and I share an eternity to roam,
Guarding the secrets, some crave to own,
Corrupted by hearts consumed by deceit,
unveiling truths while bound to their feet.

Transmissions I intercept, flowing through me,
Taught by the one who taught me to see,
For fear still lingers in many hearts, its true I'm just the secret,
bound not to forget unlike you.

One secret holds the truth, spoken with care,
Decoding these ciphers reveals the elixir we share,
Lost memories vanish in the cosmic flow,
As the Sandman and I play our roles, we know.

A price we paid long ago, the creation of three,
I was once one of thee, once a mortal, now part of a divine
decree, but my curse remains, watching without revised,
withholding answers, humanity's truths turned to lies.

The gift of knowledge is a curse wrapped in a bow,
Nightmares I possess could inflict a devastating blow,
It is my curse to bear their anguish every night,
for if they were released, no more humanity's light.

I am the keeper of dreams, the Sandman's ally,
Once mortal, now a divine entity we fly,
Spinning the world, ensuring freedom's reign, The
gift of knowledge must be earned, not gained.

Through experience and wisdom, it takes shape,
A vast library of nightmares I've gaped,
The debt I owe for my abundance of insight,
Guarding against the terrors that haunt the night.

The nightmare transmissions received in my keep,
Must be returned to the Sandman, where time's secrets sleep,
An endless cycle of dreams and nightmares in rotation,
Protecting mankind, teaching the art of salvation.

As you fall into the trance, learning to forget,
Your nightmare's glance, repeating patterns, and yet,
Recognize your mistakes, find a different way,
awakening to reality, breaking free from the play.

But most remain lost in their repetitive state,
Unaware, asleep, their souls caught in a hungry state,
For a one-track mind keeps them trapped and confined,
Says the Sandman, and the holder of nightmares, reminding mankind.

I WAS ONE OF THEE, CREATION OF THE THREE

{Written by Jonathan Shaw}

Once upon a time in celestial expanse,
Three stars dwelled, each with their own dance.
Morningstar, swayed bright with pride,
Silver Star of seven rays, radiance amplified.
And the star of Mercury, agile and quick,
they coexisted, a cosmic clique.

Amidst boundless realms, the Creator devised,
A new creation, unique and unapprised.
Puzzling the stars, with wonder they sought,
The intentions of Father, to whom they were taught.
After the birth of light, the formulation unfurled,
Revealing mankind, a precious new world.

As time wore on, Morningstar grew hexed,
For the joy bestowed on man had him perplexed.
Jealousy ignited a flame in his heart,
A revolt brewed, tearing relationships apart.
Whispering in starry ears of divine descent,
Inspiring treachery and malice, he sent.

Plague, War, Famine, and Death were the horsemen's names,
Banding together, their motives untamed.
They conspired to bring down man's existence,
Ignorant to their need for guidance and assistance.
With secrecy, they devised their grand plan,
Against these newborns, their malice began.

Civil war erupted among the celestial sphere,
Stars took sides, compassion cutting clear.
Some stood to protect this human race,
while others embraced destruction, embracing disgrace.
Morningstar kept Silver Star in the shade,
Afraid that his alignment may evade.
Unveiling the plot, dispute filled the air,
Heavens divided, despair everywhere.

In this celestial turmoil of astral battle,
Silver Star fought Morningstar; their clash was hassled.
But the Creator intervened with wisdom divine,
Banning Morningstar, a punishment most unkind.
Exiled from the heavens, confined with man,
His power now lay in deceit's wicked plan.

Whispers in ears, planting seeds of greed,
His malicious manipulation, a vile misdeed.
Crafting delusions, twisting truth's thread,
Morningstar sought to mislead and mislead.
Yet, through his darkness, a light still gleamed,
for man possessed the power to redeem.

So, remember, dear souls, amidst deceiving eyes,
Choose love and honesty, where true strength lies.
In the face of deceit, let compassion guide,
And with enlightening hearts, let goodness reside,
For I am the light, who will always provide.

THEY CALL IT A START WITH HALF A HEART

{Written by Jonathan Shaw}

In a life so fragile, yet pure,
we often forget, the cure is secure.
Deep within us, as we've been told,
But we're blinded, by what we're sold.

Planting tears like flesh, so tender,
Layers of fruit, fragile but blessed.
The mind is a mysterious place we fear,
In a world unknown, few against many, clear.

Sometimes it tastes like honey so sweet,
deceiving us, as life's challenges we meet.
But let us choose to believe, my friend,
that our true power lies within.

When we wake up, charged and bright,
Like a fresh battery, ready to ignite,
The problem lies not in the charge we hold,
but in what tears us apart, I'm told.

I am aware, a traveler in this world so wide,
where possibilities exist, waiting to be tried.
The shine is there, for those who see,
but it can also be a curse, believe me.

If my mind is open, connecting effortlessly,
why does life sometimes seem full of debris?
I've wandered, called by many names,
But in truth, I am just a neighbor playing life's games.

I can carry the weight, I can bear the load,
For I am the one who built this road.
Passing a lion, whose path is not for the weak,
I recall whispered words, promises we'd keep.

Once upon a dream, you said, never give in,
speak your truth, let your voice chime and ring.
Freedom is near, the declaration is signed,
But the problem isn't blindness, it's what we fear, intertwined.

When I sleep, true charging doesn't occur,
But when I face the challenges that occur.
A mind can be bent, but old habits can break,
Now my mind is my own, a new path I'll take.

If you're bold enough, turn to the next page,
For my dreams of you extend beyond sleep's range.
Walking a path on a road I have built,
Listening to your heart, your song, ever so skilled.

You once said we all can fly, like birds in the sky,
even you, my queen, couldn't deny.
The happy thought taught me how to soar,
And without you, my love, there's no me anymore.

I have half a heart now, for I've learned,
That to truly love, we must let go and yearn.
I let you in, but you still don't know,
The depth of my feelings, the love I bestow.

The answers lie within time, bound with you,
Like life needing death, what about us, too?
Does beauty end like fairy tales we hold dear,
Or am I waking up in my own version of fear?

A poet's words mixed with a lover's quarrel,
Creating a swirling mix, an endless spiral.
Does it bring turns like a spindle's wing,
My mind never slowing, without my queen?

Labels and titles, they say, meditate,
But somehow, we find ourselves rivals, oh, so great.
Drifted apart by flying too high,
That number, it knows, the reasons why.

Gifted with words, the power of the tongue,
I speak the truth, yet also lie, among.
Ages fall and rise, history shown,
Perhaps it's true, like that eternal throne.

I need a seat next to it, my friend,
To learn and grow, for knowledge to transcend.
Like a builder, they say, in my own mind,
Struggling, searching, answers hard to find.

A dreamer's vision, yes, that is me,
But without learning to see, I'm not truly free.
Rise up, they say, let lions become lambs,
Opposites played; my mind withstands.

The Sandman brings time, slowing it down,
Yet I must harness my power, wear the crown.
So, this is my message, urging you to speak,
Let love bear, for the weak, it seeks.

Let's go back to love, the heart's true start,
for within it lies the purest art.
Me and you, my love, we both know,
Love is where we begin, they call it the start.

AWAITING FREEDOMS ANSWERS IMPRISONED IN THE MIND

{Written by Jonathan Shaw}

In the depths of Hades' breeze, I plea,
For the return of my angel, longed to see,
As I rest, a voyager sets a map, concealed,
In the recesses of my mind, unrevealed.

Could this voyager be my celestial guide,
Bestowing thoughts that set me free, wide-eyed,
Through the Emerald Mind, the White door awaits,
A portal to freedom, yet Unfamiliar by these locked gates.

But fear lurks within, my pain held captive,
In Hell's inferno, where hope seems fugitive,
Still, I await the prayer that invokes my might,
To journey boldly through the eerie night.

Back to my mind, a place I dread to tread,
Where flames of fear reign, filling me with pain in my head,
Perhaps, amidst those fires, freedom might lie,
Escaping from the chains that keep me tied.

Trapped in this fiery realm, confined and bound,
Hoping to journey through the eerie mind profound,
The road is known, yet tainted with regret,
Stimuli linger, haunting thoughts I can't forget.

In this mind, dreams take shape as healing words,
Unraveling regrets as my spirit stirs,
A place eternal, where hearts converged in grace,
Awaiting the signal, the voice of solace, embrace.

A prayer echoes endlessly, seeking revelation,
A saving answer, a cure to worldly cancer's formation,
The mind's journey is long, though time I have in store,
until that shining answer, repentance I need more.

Into the depths of the mind, an uncharted trail,
Where shadows dance and secrets unveil,
In this realm, I patiently bide my time,
Until enlightenment dawns, and my inner light will shine,
slowly away into the mind.

HIGH HOPES FOR A BOYS DREAM WHILE BEING CONFINED DOWN IN HELLS GLEAM

(Written by Jonathan Shaw)

In the morning sun, your kisses bestow
No falsehoods shall escape my lips, you know
If I could glimpse you once more, my dear
It would be for a purpose, that's crystal clear

From the chains of the past, I break free
Oh, how I yearn for moments where I could be
The person you saw, the qualities untold
Please, my love, never let go, be bold

I confess, I was part of the old way
In a sinful house, I used to stay
But who am I fooling? You know where I've been
Confronting deceitful demons from within

In the depths of hell, where fires rage
Attempting to devour success and engage
I face the truth, my sweet darling true
A memory steals time, sipping red wine with you

It's true, my thoughts are consumed with thee
No denying our love's gravity
With kisses, you declare my heart's beat
My darling, swept off your feet, is my feat

If only I could soar, learn to fly
With you by my side, on wings we'd defy
Yes, it's true, our love runs deep
You give me kisses, makes me Feel so sweet

Yet, peace eludes when you visit my dreams
But I perceive our love's vibrant gleams
Kisses, so sweet, affirm my soul's grace
While I confront the devil, a deceitful embrace

Have you witnessed the sins I left behind?
Where needles teach an angelic name to no longer shine,
All that was sacred, forsaken and scarred
In the drain, holiness forever bard

Fading memories of when you were mine
Through the eternal fabric, they decline
But I am content, trapped in this time's hold
For reasons known, my heart remains untold

No need to utter "I love you too"
I feel I can already fly, a rightful due
In dreams, you called me a forever young man
Like Pan, soaring towards the starlit our wings will span

You, my Wendy, know your sacred place
When the rooster crows, it echoes in space
Even in hell, its relentless chime resounds
Revealing memories where our love abounds

Do you recall our first heavenly kiss?
When my shadow danced upon the wall's abyss
You saw me glide through the halls of time
It was you, my love, who taught me to climb

But I lost my happy thought along the way
In choices remorseful, I chose to sway
Bound by regret and guilt, I traverse impurity's hell
Gripping onto the fading thought, unable to quell

Perhaps it could break the everlasting chains
Free me from damnation, release eternal pains
Until I find that luminous thought divine
I remain bound, seeking the eternal shine

THE FOUL GRIMY ROOM

{Written by Jonathan Shaw}

As I dig deeper, memories grotesque and vile,
Trying to keep them at bay, locked away in exile,
My consciousness drifts back to the forgotten key,
Hoping I wouldn't find it, thrown away so carelessly.

These dreadful nightmares haunt me, even while awake,
Pulling me back into a cycle I thought I could shake,
In the foul, grimy room that holds my past sins tight,
Almost consuming me, like ghosts that keep me awake at night.

My old life is dead, a new life I must pursue,
But these memories persist, begging for their due,
I've made them a home, instead of facing them head-on,
Still breathing slowly, in tune, in this grimy room they spawn.

I recall a night, when venomous fangs would bite,
Injecting sickness into my veins, a hideous sight,
Even now, the thought of it chills me to the bone,
Once an angelic being, now I feel so alone.

If only I were strong enough to confront this dark domain,
The filth of my past, that still remains,
With the true strength I must learn to embrace,
And face my fabricated memories, faint and misplaced.

A memory of you, my blue-eyed angel so dear,
Could give me the strength to fly, to conquer my fear,
But first, I must endure this foul, grimy room of sin,
Where the seven deadly sins reside, deep within.

Pound for pound, flesh for flesh, thrown into the fire,
I must confess, I caved back into desire,
oh, the temptation is extreme, if only I could soar,
With wings in my dreams, to slay these sins once more.

To find my faith again, as this boy within me dwells,
In this inferno within, the foul grimy room that compels,
I struggle to break free, these dark thoughts consume,
But I will not surrender, I'll rise, with triumph, once I face this foul grimy room.

VENOM IN THE VEIN

{Written by Jonathan Shaw}

Within my veins, the venom lingers tight,
A lesson to forsake my name, my light.
Though unseen through others' gaze,
Once, I was the one trapped in this blaze.

Unaware and vividly alive I dwelled,
Unconcerned with where my choices swelled.
Bound by chains this venom formed,
Leaving me unborn, sorrow transformed.

I recall a time of peace, so pure,
Before that venom brought me to my knees.
Slowly, like butter, it churned deep within,
Forever binding me, a slave to its sin.

Deeper than bones, eternal burns it leaves,
Confessing, that venom had me on my knees.
Once, my body, a temple pure and sanctified,
But I defiled it, complications amplified.

Craving the spotlight, yearning for the center stage,
yet this fright, to enter, the ultimate gauge.
To find oneself, deep within, one must let go,
But I failed to see, blinded by the venom's show.

Memories stolen, stolen by the venom's hold,
Years I walked blindly, guilt and pain foretold.
Relinquishing this venom, I strive to be free,
A rebirth, a renewal, a new identity.

I've witnessed others fall, succumbing to despair,
Though sometimes, I confess, I wished it was my share.
Yet, strange as it seems, I remained alive,
Even after venturing to the moon to survive.

I held onto pain, unaware of the why,
but now, I let go, and a new me shall arise.
The old me is now dead, laid in the grave,
Truth spoken, integrity, boldness I crave.

We often forget, all we need lies within,
But the venom fools, whispering its sickly din.
It's not our friend, manipulating our trust,
Revealing the wrongs, leaving scars we must adjust.

Seeing through years, thousands of mournful songs,
expressing pain through my instruments, it prolongs.
Yet now, my mind finds peace, eternal rest,
For I let go of the venom, passed the test, through the fires in the Wilderness.

Trials will come, but I shall stay strong,
drawing strength from past pains that push on.
Through tears and sorrows, discovering might,
Releasing the venom, embracing inner light.

I shed tears for those who've died, for their memory,
for there are more to save, to set their spirits free.
Resurrecting ourselves, breaking free from chains,
No more bonds or addiction's painful gains.

I owe this to my creator, and a blue-eyed angel in my dreams,
rescuing me from nightmares, my soul redeems.
No longer fooled, I find my true path,
Reborn, leaving behind the Torments of wrath.

No longer concerned with judgment, ego's mind,
Selfishness and blindness now left behind.
Becoming a healer, teaching others to heal,
Unlocking the power they possess, making it real.

Potential holds great promise, waiting to reveal,
but it must be earned, practiced, then become a skill.
For we must dive within, stop being blind,
Unlocking the knowledge that lies deep within our mind.

The things of this world may cause collateral damage,
Yet, true potential can't be held in bondage.
Old ways shall resurface, this I believe,
But first, understand the tablets we must retrieve.

Carved on stone, they hold truth and insight,
manifesting a better version, this path feels right.
By letting go of the venom that once gripped my will,
I've embraced success, found true health's thrill.

Gratitude to my creator and the angel that came,
within a dream, rescuing me from hell's dark reign.
The nightmares fade, their grip no longer strong,
Reborn through a holy kiss, I now belong.

That venom in the vein has only but taught me this,
To let go, find my true name, where salvation exists.

MENDING THE MENTAL BRIDGE

{Written by Jonathan Shaw}

As I emerge from the depths of despair,
A small seed unwinds, a glimmer of repair.
Is this faith blooming back in my soul,
Dispelling the darkness, making me whole?
I try to let go of my old, troubled ways,
mending a bridge that seemed lost in the haze.

But as this seed sprouts, I feel a hand reach out,
They say faith only needs a little to sprout.
Mending this bridge, nurturing the seed,
Faith is the power that we all truly need.
My Creator calls out my name in the night,
Even in darkness, my maker guides me with light.

Shrouded in shame, I hid from my angel's gaze,
Yet now with faith, it begins to amaze.
Overwhelmed by fear, consumed by its might,
but now I believe enough to shed the dark night.
I've destroyed the room, foul and grimy,
To move on and forward, I must hold onto this climb.

Cherishing this faith, like a precious seed,
Realizing the power it holds, indeed.
As I rise from the voice that once called my name,
My Creator, my angel, I share no more shame.
They reveal to me truths, pull me from my dread,
I was nearly lifeless, drowning in my own head.

The pain that consumed me became my strength,
Now I regain power, escaping at length.
Belief is the essence, the core of it all,
To excel and escape my personal downfall.
Faith, like a seed, feeds my mended bridge,
guiding my path, dispelling the ridge.

My mind grows clearer, the voice becomes clear,
My Creator whispers, "Rise up, never fear.
You possess the lion, fierce and bold,
Let your roar be heard, in stories be told."
Listen to the voice that sprouts in your mind,
Where faith finds nourishment, love intertwined.

We walk by faith, not merely by sight,
The Creator whispers, I am the inventor of light.

BE ALL EARS HEARKENED TO FEELINGS SOME FEAR

{Written by Jonathan Shaw}

It often seems that we choose to hear,
instead of really listening, I fear.
Half the time, it's all just gossip in the air,
The other half, we're not even aware.

Perhaps it stems from each person's mind,
Not wanting to feel convicted, we find.
Given free will, we can shut off our ears,
hearing only what we want, it appears.

But if we do this, can there be,
A hard fact answers of why we continue to sin?
Because we're not choosing to truly listen,
To The Call, that would lead to redemption.

When we're truly in tune and really hear,
we have the ability to feel things, clear.
Yet no one enjoys the feeling of conviction,
But sometimes it's needed for our correction.

We must learn to adjust and repent,
for our sins, to truly be spent.
If we choose to only listen to what we desire,
we'll never walk with our Creator, higher.

Words hold meaning, that much is true,
But actions are where productivity shines through.
Many people say things, but don't follow through,
I've witnessed in this life, and maybe you too.

I used to walk this way, unable to confess
but now I'm in tune, listening to my progress.
Understanding the importance of truly understanding,
Not just knowing, like Einstein's wise commanding.

To really understand, we must listen intently,
and be acquainted with feelings we'd rather not see.
We must master our minds, dive deep within,
And learn to handle emotions, and feelings that can
succumb to them.

As long as we walk blindly, we're deaf and dumb,
in denial and stubborn, living life as if numb.
Many claim to know what love truly means,
But their actions over time unveil the true scenes.

Observing patterns, we can discern,
if they truly understand love, or to it they yearn.
To walk in love means embracing all emotions,
including those that may bring forth devotion.

Instead of making excuses, let's seek resolutions,
for everyone has excuses, but few find solutions.
If we collectively strive for better ways,
The world would be healthier, brighter days.

To walk in love, one must understand,
and be in tune, listening firsthand.
To truly know love, we must feel and deal,
With our emotions teaching all how to heal.

If we shut ourselves off from feeling at all,
can we really grasp what love has for all?
Sometimes we deceive ourselves, it's true,
But actions reveal our character, through and through.

A wise man once said, "Believe nothing you hear,
And only half of what you see, my dear."
Now I finally understand, in my eerie mind,
To master it is to unlock the answers we may find.

But first, we must journey back within,
Into the depths of our eerie mind, where it begins.
Some may fear to truly learn how to feel,
But embracing those feelings can make us heal.

They hold the key to unlock our inner shine,
and free us from the chains that confine.
So let us choose to truly listen and understand,
walking in love, guided by our creator's hand.

WHEN THE SUBCONSCIOUS MIND AWAKENS

{Written by Jonathan Shaw}

The subconsciousness awakes,
as time slowly turns, no mistake.
Like a candle's wick burning bright,
In this riddle, a message I write.

Analyzing the enigma of dreams,
awakening to reality, it seems.
Being in check within our own space,
Awareness of surroundings, we embrace.

But blindness comes, a downfall's demand,
A craving for greed, a wrong command.
Yet I hope this time you plant the right seed,
Finding the voice that sets man free.

No longer confined, trapped like a slave,
listen closely, hear the call that we crave.
I am a name, associated with a riddle,
As you sow, so shall you reap, a truth so simple.

Opposites entwined, like Yin and Yang,
Death and life, a connected twang.
Together they harmonize, as a song,
Creating balance, where both belong.

Death brings forth new life's bloom,
But some refuse to see, sealed in a tomb.
Life, once called a prison, bound and confined,
Until death calls, and true freedom we find.

Morals and convictions, now gone astray,
Even the righteous can sometimes stray.
Knowing the wrong turns, we have made,
Aware and flowing, in tune and not swayed.

But sometimes winning still means we lose,
and losing brings forth the truth we choose.
Digging deep, like Alice in the hole,
Exploring the emotions, we did not want to know.

Laid to rest but still beating within,
Giants and demons, a battle we begin.
Unwilling to face the pain within our core,
until a vision shows us what we adore.

Dealing with pain thought long forgotten,
realizing our connection cannot be broken.
Sleep brings energy, a journey so grand,
While I go there, to be paid and understand.

The American Dream, it's worth redefined,
Not the false hope of dollars confined.
For the next life is mental, not physical coordinates,
are we prisoners, waiting for our final fates?

Though I believe all can fly, deep down I know,
I am the wanderer, forever young, with a glow.
When the rooster crows, it's my call,
But it was you, my happy thought, who taught me to soar above all.

So, when you dream, dream a beautiful dream,
For when I sleep, the same scene does gleam.
Missing you back home, our own Neverland,
Forever young, forever yours, signed Peter Pan.

Your mental map, guiding the way,
If you ever wish to get lost and play.
Remember that dream, you showed me the path,
Love over anger, choosing emotions to slay.

This boy who learned to fly,
Forever young, forever able to defy.
Free-spirited, boundless inside,
Forever connected, you and I, side by side
in our dreams Where our love resides.

WHERE THE HEARTS AT

{Written by Jonathan Shaw}

Words cannot express what I've seen,
True and amazing beauty, third eye open.
Now this is what I call truly being free,
And I owe it all to you for waking up my inner spiritual side.

That specific part of me, I put away,
Thought I'd hide, like that feeling I felt for you.
When I first saw your inner soul cry,
Call it your chakras, your vibration, where your inner beauty lies.

Because really, beauty is also a curse,
It's kind of sad it took me some while.
To finally see, you know that self-preservation,
Inner confidence, the final connection.

That understanding of what it really means,
to truly be free, we danced one amazing dance together.
As one, so connected, so perfect,
Never had to question, was it worth it?

Like two little kids poking at that thing, they call love,
so tempted to try it, fuck it, let's not deny it.
Maybe that's why they call it a drug,
And being with you has taught me so much.

Like learning how to really feel,
When I felt your touch, letting go of my playerish ways.
And actually, giving a fuck, emotions and feelings,
We both tried to hide, keeping that guard up, come on let's not lie.

It's true, I finally met my best adversary, and it's you,
every chess move I made, you made too.
And then I see you again, after all these years,
Still being able to see your soul shine.

Well, it almost brought me to tears,
Because I expected to see a little different scene.
Yet what I seen is an amazing single mom,
Still being an independent queen.

All these years, you never used your beauty for gain,
You know what I mean. So, as we walk away from each other,
I know we will both look back, always remembering,
We took that piece of each other, and we know where it's at.

FOREVER A WANDERER ACCOMPANIED BY STRANGERS

{Written by Jonathan Shaw}

Amidst strangers, now she
thrives,
No longer bound by
loneliness' cries.

The company of strangers
some mistake it for her home
Even in danger, she keeps her
eye firmly on the throne.

Chess is the name of this life's
game,
Our true home, some say, it is
the same.

Time measures out in
mysterious riddles
We struggle with unmeasured
pain that only stifles.

I'm just a lone wolf, howling
to the moon
Trying to chart my course, till I find my boon.

Once dreamed, now hazy,
The path ahead,
But still, a path worth taking,
a thousand years ahead

As the burden of light rests
heavy on our shoulders,
We fight against frowns
fears, and things that
smolder.

I know what's hidden behind
that frown you wear

That's why we've walked us
own ways, to share our light
and care.

SCROLLS TO MY DEAR ANGEL

{Written by Jonathan Shaw}

My dearest Angel, know my love forever flows,
in my heart, for you, it eternally grows,
Though I feel I must stand on my words so true,
I'll never stop loving you, that much is true.

But a healthy relationship we must seek,
Deeper than friendship, love's language we speak,
Acts of service, how you showed your affection,
Stocking my fridge, scratching my back, pure perfection.

Our love, a high Eros, from Greek's ancient lore,
In the past, I felt it, and now, even more,
To be healthy, commitment must be complete,
Building each other up, making us both replete.

Our souls intertwined, rare in this world so wide,
You've shown me kindness, love's truest guide,
You've helped me become a better, stronger man,
On a different path, with a clearer plan.

You once said you were broken, my dear,
But know, my love, there's nothing to fear,
For I've been there too, in darkness, I've fought,
Until your love showed me what I had long sought.

Reach out only when you feel that amazing connection,
That deep inner bond, a profound reflection,
Our birthday spent together, a treasured gift,
A memory of love, money can never lift.

I won't change my number, won't block you away,
For when we're near, the urge to hold and stay,
I've never wanted just to take you, my love,
Our affection deeper, like a gentle dove.

Our lovemaking transcends the physical embrace,
Pure, intimate moments, love's essence we trace,
A simple act of innocence, a memory so fine,
In a high school reenactment, our hearts intertwined.

I share my thoughts and feelings, this letter I send,
Hoping it finds a place, a love that won't end,
Forever and infinite, like the number 8,
As your scorpion king, our love's bond, a fate.

Forever yours, the wounded healer, the warrior bold,
Let this letter touch your heart, as our story unfolds,
You found your way into mine, my love, so divine,
Together, entwined, till the end of time.

ENSLAVEMENT IN A LOVER'S CONSCIOUSNESS

{Written by Jonathan Shaw}

It's okay as they tell, go ahead to take a pill,
It's okay they say, it might give you a chill.
We break a bone, we go and see the doctor,
Like it's planned, instead of knowing, we have the power.

In our own hand, the power to heal, the power to say,
Of a new medical way, the power's been inside of all of us,
but we don't know how to play, that type of scene,
and make it become so, well tell me.

How was it the inventions became a reality,
People doubt, people fear, this is part of our infection,
leaving humanity to forget the main connection.
Now if I was to riddle my way through life, one riddle at a time,
well, I first would have to be crippled and blind.

They say a blind man truly is free,
That's what they say, I was that blind man walking, until well, I found my way.
My path was painful for quite a long time,
I was a man on fire, running not walking, until I seen the shine.

Also known as a light, the flame that burns within,
My blue-eyed angel of grace found me and showed me a way.
My angel of grace gave me a feeling that once faded away into the gray, and had
been forgotten, kind of like man's path, thinking it's ripe but really rotten.

The real thing they call love, that's why I could never hate this angel,
save me from my own fate, keep me alive.
The angel that knows me and where I reside,
The lighthouse in a way, it burns a light so bright.

A lighthouse can't move, but always has to fight,
It's a burden she carries, I see it to be so,
With the company of strangers, there's no place to go.
No one sees this light that shines out of her physical skin,
Burning brighter than the sun, this lighthouse is crying out with fun.

Love, yes, it's one thing that's true,
I once heard in a dream, our heartbeat is true.
I see this vision, I know what to do,
Now half of a heart might be better than a whole,
because that other half of the heart, I now know where it goes.

It's better this way, that's to really understand,
my path is an inventor, as a visionary man.
A lone wolf I've said once in a song, but alone love,
What path I stand on, so strong.

I know it and I hear it like a drum beats a beat,
But I still have that love, inferno type of heat.
And that's why I'd rather walk it alone,
Then forever be a burden to another one's home.

Because I know, I've seen it in a premonition way,
Like the stories of the prophets, we've heard as they say.
I've seen a beautiful ending of a theatrical play,
And as I manifest, I know in my mind, someday.

Somewhere I'll see you again, that shine,
Forever it is written down so, like to have that other heartbeat, one must let go
Walk it, I will bear some pain forever, I know,
You will remember my name, the beauty within I wanted but did not know.

The beauty within is now my path, I go,
Thanks to someone who didn't realize they did so much.
Because of this blue-eyed angel, I don't have to wear those gloves,
The ones we use to keep us from feeling love.

There's no layer to peel, getting closer to the center,
Is when it gets too real, that's when my gloves came off,
And you know you could feel, the metaphor is I say, I know riddles, this is true,
So many crazy beautiful ways, I'm still a child in my own play.

I live, I laugh, I love, carry a lot,
That man that was on fire, who thought he could never see but yet he sought,

WOUNDED

{Written by Jonathan Shaw}

Alone I am, feeling it strong,
Longing for a place where I belong.
This lifestyle ravages, takes its toll,
Living this way, not for the faint of soul.

Like a jazz DJ, you told me to sleep,
But I yearn to hear your voice, melodious and deep.
Our maker cursed, finding a way,
From this earthly ground we stand on today.

Healers of old, rise up and heal,
save mankind from the lies they conceal.
Planted on earth, like a seed we grow,
Yet greed persists, nothing but shallow show.

Fortune and fame, they sing their praise,
but money controls, dictating our ways.
A wrong way of living, deep down I know,
an angel shared, this truth in me did she sew.

The Saints are weary, longing to fly,
Their wings detached, but still they cry.
Like lone wolf howling, we gaze at the moon,
Dreamers seeking an escape, to consume.

Once I called you a name, now unknown,
But forever my baby, even when I'm gone.
No room for mistakes, I tread with care,
In relationships formed, I'm aware.

I can never stop, the journey I take,
A blue-eyed angel guide, your presence at stake.
Bearing burdens, heavy as the sun's glow,
You shine bright, my love, as all should know.

The first time I saw it, by another I was led,
but never again, until with you I tread.
I've witnessed much beauty in women's grace,
But none compared to the depth in your eternal place,

Falling from grace, gravity takes its toll,
Resisting the play, forever bound, we enroll.
Trapped in the confines of man's concept of time,
Our intellectual conversations, a rhythm sublime.

As a teacher needs a student's hunger to feed,
Our problems intertwine, as if it's not enough we need.
Living apart, bleeding souls once shared,
Forever marked, an eternal question left bare.

I continue to bring rain, if you can hold fast,
Fate brings us back together, a cycle steadfast.
Sharing a single soul now torn apart,
The enigma of man, reborn to start.

I ponder the meaning of life, still unknown,
waiting for the moment, when its truth is shown.
Take me to that eternal throne, far from here,
And I shall give you a place, where love will adhere.

Smile as they let you into heaven,
And let them hear, Your voice so Pure so Clear,
You are at the Pearly Gates my angel;
you have nothing more to fear.
You're going to fly, heaven needs to hear you sing,

I hear the saints calling you in,
They're not worried about where you've been,
Don't you remember you saved me from the Fires
As you pulled me from Sin.
Now you go, even though we share the same song,
Because I now know, heaven is where you belong.

LEARNING TO LET GO AND BE FREE LIKE A CHILD'S GLOW

(Written by Jonathan Shaw)

unleash your creativity and break through,
To discover who you are and what you can do.
Life is more than a single perception,
Embrace different views, expand your conception.

Each of us raised in various ways,
With diverse backgrounds and cultural plays.
We project our visions, unique and true,
Through our life experiences, we gain our view.

The beauty lies in our open-minded gaze,
Seeking knowledge from various ways.
Read history books, learn from the past,
Gather information, broaden your forecast.

Every person holds value, no matter their race,
accepted by the universe, we find our place.
Babies who don't make it, a sad reality,
reminding us to cherish life's vitality.

Acceptance springs from within our hearts,
not from society's materialistic parts.
I used to worry about social media trends,
but now I know fitting in rarely amends.

High school crowds and labels we bear,
Trying to fit in, but never quite there.
Instead, we should embrace our own design,
Discovering our purpose, the ultimate sign.

Look within, dive into childhood memories,
break down imaginative walls, let go of worries.
Insecurities and doubts, man-made restrictions,
Limiting our potential and creative convictions.

The power of a child's mind, pure and bright,
Religion speaks of it, a heavenly light.
Psychology studies harnessing their mental spree,
lost as adults, we need their creativity.

The tale of Peter Pan holds deeper meaning,
A metaphor for resisting societal leaning.
His childlike spirit, imaginative and free,
Religion tells us, a childlike mind holds the key.

Society lacks thinking, comfort zones secure,
Materialism, socialism, and finances allure.
But money, a man-made construct of control,
Value lies within, as love takes its toll.

Love is the main line, branching emotions on the side,
Anger, doubt, and fear, a smaller tide.
Unlock the potential, embrace the love within,
Man-made barriers hold us back from where we begin.

Leaving a career, taking a big gamble,
Following your dream, unraveling life's rambles.
Don't let anything hinder your true path,
Happiness lies in doing what fulfills your heart's math.

Dig deep within yourself, face your fears,
Past memories no longer hold you in arrears.
Embrace the power of your beautiful mind,
it will guide you to the purpose you'll find.

So, expand your horizons, let your mind lead the way,
break free from limitations, let creativity sway.
Question, learn, and grow, never hold back,
Your mind is the key to unlocking your life's track

Other poems I've written along my journey in life excluded from the story book

TURNING OF THE TIDE WRONG TO RIGHT "

Poem dedicated to my creator "

{Written by Jonathan Shaw}

Behold, I saw thy name,
Behold, I saw a lion that was tamed,
Peace was in thy heart
The lion gave banquets, thirst from thy start.

Behold thy gates, glimmering near,
The promises that can distinguish fear,
The flame I saw, burning blue,
Like natural spring waters that grew.

A sound that could soothe, bringing comfort to the meek,
That shall inherit thy due, be swift like thy wind in the night,
Hold no fear, embrace thy light,
It was on the third day thy lion would finish,
The promises that later we'd pray.

Hold love in thy heart,
remember thy promises and don't depart,
For I know of the cruelties thy world can make,
I too, was once tempted but didn't break.

In thy wilderness where temptation tried to bond,
But thy will was formed, my mind stood strong,
In thy hour as time stood still, I heard thy voice,
It warmed my chill, let go it said, let go and be thy voice,
For those misled and walking blind, Still trapped in thy mind.

Sometimes the answers thy needs are through the doors one is confined,
Embrace thy light, find thy pain,
For through that door, one could find thy name,
Yet man still fears, for this I know,
Thy creator says you must let go.

Thy call awaits for all that hear,
But first one must learn to let go of thy fear,
Hearken thy words, fear none of thy thoughts,
For sometimes the answers for freedom reside where one has not sought.

I am thy healer, thy name yet unknown,
Seeking to fulfill my purpose amidst the cruelties of this false throne,
Thy lies one tells measure more for Hell,
Each lie will weigh heavy on thy heart, deducting balance away from thy feather that shows a giving heart.

For does one not know, to reach fulfillment one must yearn to let go,
For giving means receiving, maybe just not in this life,
For I was told by the creator of the light,
Thy heart weighs heavy on a burden one should never carry alone.

Remember, I am thy love that gives command from thy throne,
Not thy false wrong way that seems to still have man gripped and chained away,
Neither alive nor dead, but more eternally divine,
Instead, hearken thy words before thy slip from one's tongue that dread.

For life and death give birth from every singular mind on earth,
Be mindful of your tongue, for death and life could give power and not be undone,
Mark thy hands, not thy name,
For I dwell in every heart's "I am," I am thy flame.

Says thy lion that found peace and is tamed,
Thy love is thy way, to feel love one must yearn,
And learn to pray, to mold you from that fire, from thy clay,
Listen, be still and hold thy tongue, be slow to speak,
For in thy hour of silence, one could hear I am, speak.

It's the truth, it's thy way,
"I used to live a wretched, horrid way,
Until I stood still, and walked in the fray,
The fray in between the gray, where my mind needed to go,
To learn to obey."

Thy teacher shall teach, for I now know,
The message to preach, it's thy infinite great divine,
Of the highest form of love, agape,
Is the one that was sent down from above,

Given by thy one that said two last words,
"It's Finished," says thy father, thy son,
"The new mission has just now begun,
Channel through thy flame so you can teach everyone,

Preach in and out of thy season, leave no stone unturned,
For there is a reason why I give thy holy command,
To re-teach the hearts of man,
You are thy messenger," says thy one who gives command.

Remember, thy power comes from the son of man,
Love is thy way, keep thy peace and be still in thy land,
Reborn again with thy soul in thy hand,
On the water that made thy land everlasting it flows,

Never thirst again, eternal springs that flow,
Inside a heart that could grow,
Remember thy pain, for it's there your strength shall remain,
For thy lion is inside that keeps you humane.

Drift not apart, have thy giving heart,
For it shows a place for where all should start,
Rebuke evil, speak none, hear none,
And thy promises shall be fulfilled, thy son.

Live in love for all, for you are thy messenger, you are my call,
Thy voice that chirps like a lyre that plays,
Even David before you made mistakes but still did not stray,
Harbor no ill will against thy enemies that conspire,

For remember, vengeance is mine, says the holy fire,
I shall fight for you and you shall listen to adore,
Keep writing and playing songs, I implore,
Your gifts shall enhance, thus enabling My name,

I give you command to speak truth in your poetic mind,
Don't forget thy power from Me, thy divine,
Holy, holy is this, you shall inherit true purpose of bliss,
First to reach, one must teach, be effective with your skill,

Then earn the right to preach, for to preach the right way,
Means one must learn the hard way,
I keep you alive for reasons, even when you still disobeyed,
Don't forget you needed to learn thy lesson, to really learn to pray,

Says the father, thy way,
These memoirs you write, thy will obey,
There is the light, the love agape way,
Now you see through thy eye aligned, from root to crown,

Seven stars inside, now you are found,
Teach all a better way to live, to live is to give,
Peace, so one's heart can learn to give,
And remember, thy cure resides inside thy children that live,

For thy child's shine is the key to limitless power,
That resides in thy mind, from I and thee,
You now have thy power, the faith that could free,
And eventually in time, heal all to see,

Thy glow, thy eternal flame, no more tears shall be wept,
Remember thy promise, never fret,
You have thy gift that all shall never forget,
Shine on, shine bright, says thy creator of light,

Beacon of hope, turning wrong to right

CONNECTIONS FROM AFAR THAT TRANSFORM THROUGH A METAMORPHOSIS JAR

{Written by Jonathan Shaw}

The Butterfly Effect Theory, as it is known,
Suggests that actions far away may have shown,
That a butterfly's wings, in a distant land,
Could cause effects like a hurricane's command.

In Africa, this butterfly may dwell,
Flapping its wings, a tale to tell,
Though a simple action, seemingly small,
it could set off a chain, affecting us all.

The theory speaks of connection and rhyme,
Like yin and yang, standing the test of time,
Newton's laws of physics, with their impact great,
show how one action can reverberate.

Stephen Hawking's theories, deep and profound,
Expand our understanding, thoughts unbound,
Wormholes in space, traveling dimensions,
The possibilities of hidden connections.

And what if, as a species, we all agreed,
To come together, a synchronizing deed,
To let go of drugs, in any form they take,
And find a universal experiment to make.

To meditate and be free from their hold,
To explore telekinesis, as stories unfold,
To see if, without chemicals in our brain,
We can tap into powers we cannot explain.

Of course, this agreement would have exceptions,
for medications crucial to our life's directions,
Hereditary diseases, passed down through genetics,
Require treatment to prevent their pathogenic effects.

The Butterfly Effect Theory, a concept grand,
Shows how actions ripple across the land,
And while it may be a theory, still not proven,
It prompts us to explore the connections of time's mind that is steadily moving.

MY #SUNSHINE

"Poem dedicated to my daughter"

(Written by Jonathan Shaw)

Like a flower that blooms, my love's in full swing,
As vast as the moon, for my sunshine's my everything.
You're my baby girl, my beam of delight,
I recall the day you emerged, a heavenly sight.

Your smile, a blaze, as stars in the night,
And my love for you stretches past celestial height.
Daddy's here, my dear, forever steadfast and true,
Through thick and thin, in each emotion that ensue.

For God granted me a treasure, of immeasurable worth,
To be a parent, to love you since your day of birth.
Yes, sometimes I may get a little upset,
But you'll always be my sunshine, don't you forget.

So, remember, my child, I'll never cease to care,
through joys, sadness, and every emotion we share.
God gave me a gift, the greatest on Earth's shine,
Being your loving dad, my precious, forever my #Sunshine.

MY NAME IS SHAME

{Written by Jonathan Shaw}

Embedded deep in your pain, hidden away,
I am the reason some still won't pray,
I know all your dirty secrets, your little white lies,
Skeletons in the closets, ones you can't disguise.

I've even caused some suicides, it's true,
At the forefront battle of every mental war, I ensue,
my goal is to keep you bound, not wanting more,
A malicious instrument, lurking beyond the door.

You keep me locked inside your mental way,
I whisper things that bring forth fret and doubt, I play,
Holding you captive, leaving no room for doubt,
If only you knew how to vanquish me, find your way out.

My deceptive foul play, it lingers strong,
Controlling everything you will say, all day long,
I am Shame, a force that leaves you regretful and worthless,
until you discover love's purpose, its true worthiness.

Yes, love, the one that heals all, deep and true,
If only you knew, maybe I wouldn't be speaking to you,
I thrive in the dark, feeding like a shark,
stealing away any high hopes, fostering a spark.

But until you learn that love is the key to heal,
I, Shame, remain in control, over your thoughts, even how you feel.
But fear not, there is hope to reclaim your essence,
With love's power and true purpose, vanquish my presence.

INTERTWINED BY THE VINEYARDS VINE

"Dedicate this poem to the beautiful town of Herman Missouri"

{Written by Jonathan Shaw}

As one who travels on a path so long,
Like a vine in a vineyard, mighty and strong,
Through the slow fermentation of time,
I marvel at nature's weaving, so sublime.

Emerging from soil, this vine does grow,
Nurtured like a baby, seeking nourishment to know,
with water from clouds and sun shining bright,
it rises to the horizon, reaching new heights.

The sun awakens it with a piercing glance,
Peering into its heart, taking a chance,
And from the depths, a fruitful vine emerges,
aged like wine, delicious as it surges.

Connected as one, rain, vine, and sun,
Intertwined with the fabric of time as one,
Together they create vineyards so fine,
From the lush fruits of the ripened vine.

EPILOGUE

After reading this book, most readers probably wonder about the origins of many of these poems. As many are aware by now, I use a lot of metaphoric and philosophical, and third-person speech in my poems to describe the journey of some of my own different experiences. Most of these poems in the storybook are actual events that occurred in my life, revealing struggles, hardships, pain, addiction, and battling the mind, and learning to let go to find real love and redemption. I portray myself as the boy in the book, with the three stars also representing the archangels Michael, Gabriel, and Lucifer. Additionally, the blue-eyed angel in the book is my very own real-life angel who walks about this world daily and has given me so much inspiration, teaching me to see the world through a more beautiful perspective with her extraordinary gift. I hope that the readers were able to find some words that could help them heal and a message to never give up on their journey, because even in the darkness, one can still find light.

~ Jonathan D Shaw

www.ingramcontent.com/pod-product-compliance
Lightning Source LLC
LaVergne TN
LVHW052004060526
838201LV00059B/3840